Terms and Conditions

LEGAL NOTICE

The Publisher has strived to be as accurate and complete as possible in the creation of this report, notwithstanding the fact that he does not warrant or represent at any time that the contents within are accurate due to the rapidly changing nature of the Internet.

While all attempts have been made to verify information provided in this publication, the Publisher assumes no responsibility for errors, omissions, or contrary interpretation of the subject matter herein. Any perceived slights of specific persons, peoples, or organizations are unintentional.

In practical advice books, like anything else in life, there are no guarantees of income made. Readers are cautioned to reply on their own judgment about their individual circumstances to act accordingly.

This book is not intended for use as a source of legal, business, accounting or financial advice. All readers are advised to seek services of competent professionals in legal, business, accounting and finance fields.

You are encouraged to print this book for easy reading.

Table Of Contents

Foreword

Chapter 1:
What About Affiliate And Niche Marketing

Chapter 2:
Making Your Way With Blogs

Chapter 3:
Supplying Information

Chapter 4:
Software And Memberships

Chapter 5:
Services And Network Marketing

Wrapping Up

Foreword

Home business is the way the globe is going to go in the close future. Gone are the days when individuals knuckled down over their office desks. This is the age where the conception of career liberalization is truly going to gain ground.

Are you going to be a piece of it as early as you are able to or are you going to hold off and watch till everybody has tried it out first?

The ideal way is to get into this as quick as possible and make a name for yourself in the home business genre as soon as you are able to.

This eBook has all the knowledge you would require to launch a business from the comfort of your own home!

Work At Home Methods Unleashed
Discover Numerous Ways To Make Money From The Comfort Of Your Own Home

Chapter 1:
What About Affiliate And Niche Marketing

Synopsis

Affiliating with businesses in order to market them isn't a fresh idea. But what you have to know here is that it may make you a millionaire and you would not even have to physically adventure an inch out of your home.

What are individuals on the Net mainly looking for? Data, that's right! If you supply them the data they are looking for, you are a winner the whole way.

Great Info To Get You Going

If anybody was asked to name one technique that marketers utilize to make a surefire rapid profit on the Net, then most of them would give you the same answer - "affiliate marketing".

Though there are dozens of home business models on the Net, it is quite safe to state that affiliate marketing has to rank inside the top 3, or perhaps even at the top of the heap.

Fundamentally, the affiliate marketing model means to promote somebody's product over the Net. You're assisting them with their advertising and are getting paid a commission for that.

You are able to begin by making an account on an affiliate network like the Hydra Network (http://www.hydranetwork.com/). This is a place where advertisers post their advertising needs.

When you are a part of this network, you are able to pick out the products you wish to market. These are products of individuals inside the network.

Once you are finished with that, you'll need an affiliate marketing service to market the products you have chosen on the Net. The best in that category is Google Adwords (<http://adwords.google.com/>).

You simply have to begin a campaign here, mentioning the product you require to market and give the URL that you're advertising. Adwords will mechanically search for the correct site matches for the product and will advertise on them.

The pay is fantastic. You get paid for each click that your ad gets. This is known as Pay Per Click (PPC). All the same, there are some affiliate networking sites, like the Hydra Network we have mentioned here, that pay only when a sale is accomplished. In this case, it becomes a Pay Per Sale (PPS) affiliate service.

Your only disbursement is in beginning the Adwords campaign. All the same, here you are able to bid on how much you wish to spend. Therefore, you're actually altering your expense. The returns, but, are much more than whatever cash you will put into the business.

Niche

What's a niche content web site, in the first place? A niche content web site is a site that panders to a certain group of individuals. Like gardening is a niche; cooking is a niche; motor repair is a niche.

Others would not be interested in reading about these subjects. However, individuals who are interested in these subjects will certainly pack your site and even come repeatedly to look for fresh info that you must put up day in and day out.

There may be a niche inside a niche. Like, in gardening, there may be a sub-niche of how to do away with aphids or how to utilize the right mix of fertilizers to make those grapes larger. These are sub niches.

You have to remember one thing here... the narrower you're making your niche, the lesser is the number of individuals you are getting for your web site, but at the same time, these individuals are more centered and they will be more mattered to in doing business with you.

Think about it. If somebody truly wants to have a little info on aphid removal, they are not going to find too many web sites on it.

If your web site has that content and likewise promotes some product relating to it, like an aphid spraying, the likelihood of that visitor purchasing the product from your web site is indeed elevated.

This is the way you have to go about it.

First of all, think of a popular niche that you would like to establish a web site on. You may go to places like Google Suggest (<http://suggest.google.com/>) and check out what many individuals are looking for.

Google Suggest will likewise give you a host of keywords that you are able to utilize. These are the keywords that individuals are popularly searching.

Establish content. You'll need to have at least fifty pages or so of material to make some sort of impact. Spruce up these materials by using correct keywords so that it reaches out to the individuals who are looking for the particular information.

Then, look for products on your affiliate network web site to promote on your niche web site. Refer to chapter 1 on how to get to be a member of an affiliate network web site.

You are able to put advertisements in the form of text and banners. By having your own web site, you are saving cash on advertising services like Google Adwords. You have to popularize your web site so that more individuals visit, which in turn will step-up the number of clicks (and sales) that you get. At the same time, the popularity of your ads will step-up the prospect of your site.

Chapter 2:
Making Your Way With Blogs

Synopsis

Really few models are as popular nowadays as the business blogging model. This is one model where individuals entertain themselves by networking with others, build on their knowledge and, naturally, build on their business leads.

So, aren't you blogging already?

The one matter about blogging that you need to understand is that you are able to monetize it in a lot of different ways. There isn't simply a single way in which you are able to make cash out of a blog; there are many.

Once you have a blog of your own, it is a learning experience in itself. However, at the same time, the cash begins flowing in almost at once, which motivates you into milking your blog further.

Blogging

Blogging started out as a means of conveying personal thoughts, then it bit by bit became a publicity tool for stars and paparazzi and eventually, it reached the entrepreneurs of this globe. With marketing becoming more and more competitive, campaigning through the internet ensured that blogging research achieves new peak.

Blogging has come a long way from easy web pages to exceedingly sorted and read material of the net. Comments on blogs and the speed of passing blog links amidst users with similar interest show the might of blogging and its popularity on a global podium.

There are plenty of advantages of blogging for little, big businesses and even the non-trade sections like awareness-creating organizations worldwide. Surveys demonstrate that individuals prefer to trust those companies more, which lean towards engaging in blogging.

A Really great platform to construct your blog would be WordPress (<http://www.wordpress.com/>) or Blogger (<http://www.blogger.com/>).

These are blog programs, i.e. you are able to produce your blog utilizing the software they supply. In addition, you'll likewise need some hosting space and domain name to get your blog up and running.

The unrivaled difference between WordPress and Blogger is that Blogger is a free of charge tool. That means, you will have to contend

with ads from others on your blog. WordPress is considered to be more centered and speaks better of the commercial blogger's intents.

A different blogging service that you may like is Typepad (<http://www.typepad.com/>).

Typepad is an uploading and hosting service. You simply pay them, construct your blog through WordPress, and Typepad will take care of the uploading and hosting. One fringe benefit is that Typepad does a lot of SEO for you, so you are able to be certain that your blog will begin ranking high right from the beginning.

If you get great content on your blog (including keyword optimized text, video recordings and pictures), you are able to be certain that it will get populated soon. The search engines adore blogs because they get a regular update of content and because so many individuals continue visiting them. In today's scenario, blogs are more effective in sites.

The following are a few ways in which you are able to monetize your blog:-

- You may utilize pay-per-click advertising on your blog.
- You may directly sell or promote products.
- You may give away an eBook or an e-zine subscription and get leads.
- You may build a blog, populate it and then sell the whole thing for a respectable profit.

Chapter 3:
Supplying Information

Synopsis

Aright, we won't go into the cliché about the net being an info superhighway.

But isn't it just that?

You can't deny that! Information products are the Internet-age term which implies the publication of information-rich material on the net. This material may take any form, but broadly when we speak about information products, we're talking about eBooks, e-zines, videos, audio-books and the like.

Commonly, this is material that individuals may download and store on their hard disk and withdraw it afterwards according to their convenience. There's one more common strand running through all the information product devices - they have to furnish beneficial content to the user.

Supplying Information

There are 2 ways in which you are able to get into the information product business:-

You may produce the information content yourself or outsource it to somebody so that you have your own product to distribute.
You may promote another person's product on your site or blog.

Either way, you're doling out informative material.

One of the ways to give out this material is through affiliate marketing. If you're going to market products of others, you may select the available products from an affiliate network and distribute it through a service like Adwords.

In this case, you would not have to have your own site or blog even. All the same, you may likewise distribute such a product directly. Selling makes a great option if your product is great quality. Utilizing techniques such as search engine optimization, viral marketing, social networking and such, you may establish a brand presence for your product and gather a market for it. Once that is produced, you will discover that your product begins earning for you an everlasting stream of income.

If you hold your own product, there are a lot more benefits. Number one, individuals associate you with somebody who is an authority in the subject. Your name in the byline means a lot for your believability.

This will ensure that your additional products get a niche for themselves too. Now, bearing your own product doesn't mean that you have to sit and produce stuff yourself. You could outsource work really easily.

On jobsites like GetAFreelancer (<http://www.getafreelancer.com/>) and ScriptLance (<http://www.scriptlance.com/>), it's really easy to discover professionals who'd work for you at an attractive price, and give you the rights of their work.

For video recording material, you may publish interesting video recordings on YouTube (<http://www.youtube.com/>) and combine their impact with a different product that you're selling. Your video supplies individuals with great information and at the same time supplies a link from where they may download an eBook that you're marketing. That way, you are able to combine your marketing efforts and acquire added advantages.

Achieve the maximum mileage out of your information product enterprise. If you're looking to stick to your net home business for a long time, you'll have a presence on the net, and nothing works better than information products for that.

Chapter 4:

Software And Memberships

Synopsis

Never undervalue the might of software applications. You are utilizing dozens of them on your desktop yourself. A software may make you wealthy... really wealthy. Ever heard of somebody named Mr. Gates?

Membership web sites may lead in a lot of individuals through the door of your net business enterprise. What's more is that these individuals may be with you forever and a day.

Some Great Ways To Break In To The Business

Selling software packages is among the most forceful routes to make great income on the net. Individuals who utilize computers are constantly attempting to make their jobs simpler or to add more quality to their jobs. That's the reason they're looking for great software all the time.

With broadband net, it has become so very simple to supply software in downloadable formats. You market a link from where individuals may download a particular software package and allow them to access it when they make payment. They'll pay and you provide them the link to download the software package.

A lot of marketers tease individuals by presenting them demo versions of the software free of charge. This lets the downloaders comprehend the caliber of the product before they choose to spend good cash on it.

These demo versions typically have a few features locked or they're timed demos which expire after an hour's worth of utilization or so. When that occurs, individuals are prompted to purchase the product to take advantage of it limitlessly.

So, what must this software package be like? Individuals on the net like each and every sort of software. Or, let us put that in a different way - each and every type of software package on the net will find takers. There's a niche for everything on the net.

So, if you've made a software application that will help granny remember her recipes or made a software package that will help a businessman with his end-of-the-year account statement, you're going to find humans who will be willing to download that and check it out. The success rests in the marketing.

For marketing, you are able to utilize more of the same techniques that you have been utilizing right along. If your software package becomes prominent, particularly in places where your niche market commonly visits, you may be assured of a healthy flow of down-loaders.

At the same time, you have to remember that there's no lifespan for this. There will constantly be down-loaders, provided you market well and keep upgrading your software package, which means, you are able to continue generating a flow of passive revenue through this.

You don't need to have your own software application either. You may purchase the resell rights of software package and sell it. There are a lot of creative individuals on the net who like building software but don't like the promotion aspect of it. These individuals give away the software they've developed for a price.

You are able to modify these software packages to an extent and in a few cases you are able to rebrand them too. Naturally, you sell them at a much higher and enduring price than you purchased it for. The accompanying are a few sites from where you are able to purchase resell rights of software:-

Jimmy's Value World
      (<http://www.jvwinc.com/network/offering.html>)

Rebrand Software
(<http://www.rebrandsoftware.com/>)

You may simply seek 'software re-sell rights' on Google to determine a host of other such sites.

Membership sites are simply what their name suggests - these are sites where you're asking individuals to become members of a web site and in return you're supplying them with a host of value-added services. These individuals are the members of the web site, which is something of the kind of a net club where they enjoy particular privileges.

On many membership sites, the members are supplied with some free of charge offers and downloads and they acquire privileges on assorted affiliate sites as well. A lot of social networking sites are likewise membership sites.

There, you become a member so that you are able to acquire access to network with others. There are gobs of game membership sites as well, where the advantage of becoming a member is that you are able to play games - which may be free online versions or downloadable versions that you may acquire at a lower price.

The general concept of a membership site is that you keep your treats hidden from the basic net public and allow them access to it only if they've taken the membership action that you ask them to.

This action may be filling in a net form, with or without payment, authoring an email to you to express their desire to join the web site and so forth.

Even if you don't actively demand payment, you're building a relationship. You're getting a list of leads, to which you are able to market your additional commercial efforts.

But, you have to understand that membership sites do take much effort. You have to have an unparalleled concept to make your membership site a hit and you have to make regular efforts to provide superior material to your members.

They're going to be frustrated otherwise and you're going to lose all the potential you've built. A failed membership site is a huge disgrace in the Internet marketing domain. It may eat into your additional prospects also.

But, if you have the passion and the ardor for it, go right ahead and establish a membership site. You'll soon be hobnobbing with numerous individuals having your like tastes and interests. And, you'll be making a great sum of money through it also.

Chapter 5:
Services And Network Marketing

Synopsis

What's the most beneficial, most unparalleled and special thing that you are able to sell and keep selling eternally? Your own services, that's what. You have a gift for something? Go right ahead and pitch it on the net. You'll see the earnings pouring in.

Network marketing has been present since the pre- net times and it's received its share of raves and rants. All the same, this is a lucrative route as is clearly evidenced by the 1000s of millionaires it has bred at a worldwide level.

What Talent Do You Have

The net has a market for everything. Even for your own services. If you believe you're great at something, the net may be the most beneficial place for you to peddle your skills. There are individuals seeking all sorts of services on the net.

The jobsites have made the net a closer market than any other. Individuals are seeking services, and suppliers of these services are seeking individuals who they may sell the services to. The right collaboration may mean a lot of cash to you.

Naturally, it's understood that the sort of services that have a demand on the net are services that you are able to supply online. These are by and large services related to site building and marketing. The following services are much desired:-

- Material creation
- Blog management
- SEO
- Site creation
- Social networking services like Craigslist postings
- Handling other virtual staff
- Proofing and editing

If you feel you fit inside any of these skills, you may make an astonishing sum of money with them. Remember that the net lets you reach out to a worldwide level and you may liaise with individuals from all over the Earth to seek work. The following are a few sites where you should make an account quickly so that you begin earning with this:-

- GetAFreelancer (<http://www.getafreelancer.com/>)
- ScriptLance (<http://www.scriptlance.com/>)
- Elance (<http://www.elance.com/>)
- Guru (<http://www.guru.com/>)
- EUFreelance (<http://www.eufreelance.com/>)
- ...and a lot of others.

You have to simply get moving with this and see the immense potential that dwells therein. These are all bidding sites. You discover a job that meets your tastes and then make your bid and provide an estimated time of windup. If the project poster determines that to be o.k., they'll choose you. You're paid through online routes.

The drawback here is that you must spend time. You have to be at your desktop for all the time that you're returning money, which is a really different matter from other approaches like affiliate marketing. You earn simply as much as you work and there's no scope for residual revenue.

Networking

The idea is too darned easy - you establish a network of individuals and jointly you market a product or service. At the same time, you attempt to bring more individuals into the network. For every individual that joins the network, the upline members pull in a commission.

Direct sales take in the cash too, but the chief commission is brought in through the commissions that the network building returns.

But, the execution isn't quite as easy. Building the network may be formidable to most individuals. Even so, there are a lot of facilities you get so that you are able to construct the network well.

You get a site from the network marketing company that you link up with, you are able to attend physical seminars and webinars and you've access to a host of content, online and offline, where you may learn how to market your network to the limit.

You have to remember one matter - joining a network marketing opportunity may be a life-changing experience. You may start seeing everything in an altogether fresh light. However that's the way you may bring in all those six figure incomes a month.

2 of the most popular network marketing opportunities of the globe,

Amway

(<http://www.amway.com/>)

and Herbalife

(<http://www.herbalife.com/>)

market themselves on a worldwide level. Joining such opportunities extends the awesome advantage of prevailing goodwill that you may cash in on. As well, they've their own training and orientation plans all over the world which may help you begin on the right foot.

The drawback here is that there many players in the network marketing (likewise called MLM) world.

Many of them are swindlers and these are the individuals who have given the industry a foul name. You have to especially be beware of pyramid systems in which individuals take in money only by building a network but don't have any product to distribute.

In most parts of the globe, pyramid systems are considered to be illegal and the individuals involved in such an activity may be prosecuted by the law.

Wrapping Up

So here I have provided some examples to get your home businesses up and running so that you may go to fresh levels of affluence.

Home in on the action you would like to follow up on, do a little research and set about the path you have chosen. You won't be wanting for anything before long!

There are several other ways to bring in the cash from a home business.... So do your homework and research and see what works best for you and your interests.

To your success... go out and get it!

www.ingramcontent.com/pod-product-compliance
Lightning Source LLC
Chambersburg PA
CBHW030602220526
45463CB00007B/3148